THE BODY SP Language

written by
A. W. Mausolf

illustrated by
Jennifer Soriano

Level 5

BOOK 2
Second Edition

Dedicated to the Church, including our family and friends, and especially to Mother Mary and Saint John Paul.

Tremendous thanks to all TOBET members over the years. Special thanks to Andrea, Joanna, Kathy, Sarah, Sheryl, Tamara, and Véronique. We are grateful for consultation work by the translator of the *Theology of the Body*, Dr. Michael Waldstein, as well as Dr. Susan Waldstein and Dr. Danielle M. Peters. We are also grateful for the consultation work of Katrina J. Zeno, MTS.

For my brothers: Titus, Johnny, Bernard, Tommy, and brothers-in-law: Joe and Nick

Nihil Obstat: David Uebbing, B.A., M.A.
Censor Librorum

Imprimatur: +Most Reverend Samuel J. Aquila, S.T.L.
Archbishop of Denver
Denver, Colorado, USA
July 26, 2018

Library of Congress information on file. ISBN 978-1-945845-33-8 • Second Edition

Cover Design: FigDesign • Layout: Emily Gudde • Editor: Dayspring Brock • Associate Editor: Alexis Mausolf

Excerpts from the English translation of the *Catechism of the Catholic Church*. New York: Catholic Book Publishing Co., 1994.

Based on John Paul II's *Man and Woman He Created Them: A Theology of the Body*. Trans. Michael Waldstein, Copyright © 2006. Used by permission of Pauline Books & Media, 50 Saint Paul's Ave, Boston, Massachusetts 02130. All rights reserved. www.pauline.org.

All Scripture verses are from the *New American Bible*, Revised Edition (NABRE).

Page 19: *Peanuts* by Charles Schulz © Copyright 1973 DHX Media.

Excerpt from *YOUCAT*. Trans. Michael J. Miller. (San Francisco: Ignatius Press, 2011), www.ignatius.com. Used with permission.

Printed in the United States of America. © Copyright 2021 Monica Ashour. All rights reserved. No part of this book may be reproduced or transmitted in any form or by any means, electronic or mechanical, including photocopying, recording, or by any information storage and retrieval system without permission in writing from the publisher.

Table of Contents

1 **The Body Speaks a Language** — 4
- Humans can communicate with their bodies.
- Certain bodily actions have certain meanings.
- The language of the body expresses many different emotions and responses.

2 **Telling the Truth with the Body** — 14
- We can know the truth and live it out bodily.
- Our bodies can speak truths or lies.
- Truth builds trust and thus union with others.

3 **Manners and Truth** — 26
- We can find the greatest truth to express in each situation.
- Good manners are important all around the world.
- Our bodies can speak the language of politeness.

4 **The Body Speaks in Scripture** — 38
- Scripture shows that the body speaks a language.
- The Gospel shows the goodness of telling the truth with the body.
- Jesus and Mary speak a language of love with their bodies.

The Body Speaks a Language

Universal Language

How many languages do you know? There are about 6,500 languages spoken on this earth today. Words have power and meaning. We communicate with each other by using words. Yet, did you know that language can be spoken without words? Our **bodies** speak a language too!

Gesundheit!

¡Feliz Navidad!

Grazie!

مكيلع مالسلا

שלום

Спасибо

Bon Appétit!

サヨナラ

We might not be aware of it, but our bodies are always speaking a language. We can understand a lot from what the body says.

Our bodies tell us we are **human**.
Our bodies tell us we are **old** or **young**.
Our bodies tell us we are **male** or **female**.

"...[T]he human body speaks a 'language' of which... its author is [a human], as male or female."
Theology of the Body 104:7

How Does the Body Speak?

Sometimes the language of the body is automatic. We cannot always control the language our bodies speak.

Do you ever get butterflies in your stomach around holidays or special occasions? With that tickly feeling your body says, *Get ready for something exciting!*

What about when you suddenly have to yawn? Your body is saying, *I am sleepy.*

Do you sometimes become very wiggly and restless? Your body is saying, *I have lots of energy.*

Your body has a lot to say.

If you stand on the highest diving board, looking down at the pool far below, your stomach might feel tight and your breathing might be shallow. Your heart beats fast. Your body is saying, *I am scared.*

Have you ever felt your face blush? Your body is saying, *I feel embarrassed.*

If you have to give a class presentation or meet an important person, you might stammer or feel your palms sweat. Your body is saying, *I am nervous.*

Your body communicates important things at each moment.

7

Actions Have Meanings

Without words, people around the world can understand each other through the language of the body. What is a smile? A smile shows goodwill, friendliness, peace, and even thankfulness. In other words, a smile means, *I am glad you are here.*

What does a frown say? A frown is usually a sign of disagreement, disappointment, or hostility. In other words, a frown says, *I am not happy.*

Even young children know that **certain bodily actions have certain meanings**. The human body speaks a universal, God-given language.

Let's think of some ways the body might speak. A wave of the hand is usually a greeting. Pointing a finger shows direction. Below are some more examples. Can you think of others?

Gesture	Meaning
Smile	"Nice to meet you."
Push	"Get away from me!"
Bow	"I respect you."
Frown	"I am unhappy."
Giving a Gift	"I appreciate you."
Shrug	"I don't know/understand."

© Copyright 2017 by Monica Ashour. All rights reserved.

Expressive Language

Our bodies can communicate strong feelings.

If you turn red and furrow your eyebrows, your body may be saying, *I am angry.*

If you are tense and sweating, your body may be saying, *I am anxious.*

When your face blushes, your body may be saying, *I am ashamed.*

What do the rest of these emojis say?

Loving Language

Here are some examples of how the body speaks in a loving and friendly way.

When you laugh with your friends, your body says, *We are bonding.*

When you hand something to someone, your body says, *I am giving and sharing.*

When you hug and kiss your parents, your body says, *We are family.*

When you give your friends a thumbs-up, your body says, *Good job! You did it!*

When you hold your little brother's hand to cross the street, your body tells him, *I am protecting you.*

When entering a church, you genuflect before the tabernacle in which Jesus is bodily present.

Your body is saying to Him, *You are my God. I worship and adore You.*

We don't always need words to speak. Our **bodies** speak a language too. People can understand us, and we can understand them, through bodily actions and reactions.

Have you thought carefully about what you would like your body to say? The language of the body shows who you are, inside and out!

"Truth or truthfulness is the virtue which consists in showing oneself true in deeds and truthful in words...." *CCC 2468*

Mission: See how often you can speak without words today. Offer a helping hand, a smile, or a hug to someone in your family. Show full attention with your body in school by upright posture and eye contact with the teacher. Respond with words when someone addresses you, but try to focus on what your body is saying to others today.

2 Telling the Truth with the Body

Why Tell the Truth?

Most of us have heard the tale told about young George Washington chopping down a cherry tree with his new hatchet. When his father asked angrily whether he had done this destructive thing, George bravely admitted to it: "Father, I cannot tell a lie. I did cut it with my hatchet." George preferred to be punished than to lie.

To the boy's surprise, his father took him in his arms and said that his son's honesty was worth more to him than a thousand cherry trees! We, too, can love the truth and speak it fearlessly.

"Thou shalt not bear false witness against thy neighbor" (Ex. 20:16).

Why is this commandment so important? God is the source of all truth; a lie goes against His very nature. Therefore, telling a lie harms our friendship with God.

Lying damages our character and hurts those around us. It can be a dangerous thing. It is like a tornado, building momentum. You never know when a lie will show up and cause destruction all around.

The Language of Truth

We are called to love truth and live it out always. How can we do that?

Truthful words and truthful bodily actions mirror the greatest truth of the heart. Our bodies speak truthfully when there is no contradiction between the truth that we know and the truth that we show.

If you are nervous on the dodgeball court and you show that by flinching, your body is telling the truth.

If you are happy that your team is winning and you show that by jumping in the air and cheering for them, your body is telling the truth.

The Language of Falsehood

How do we know if our actions always match the greatest truth we know in our hearts? It would be easy to tell if we were like Pinocchio. Each time he told a lie, his nose would grow longer. It is not always so obvious for us when we deceive ourselves or others.

We, like Pinocchio, can tell lies using words. But our bodies speak a language too. So our bodies can also speak lies.

Remember, **certain bodily actions mean certain things**. If we change the God-given meaning of an act or gesture, our bodies speak falsely. For instance, the true meaning of a smile is friendship and goodwill. However, if we smile while being unkind to someone, we have betrayed that meaning. It's not right to twist the body's meaning

Like a smile, laughter has deep meaning. It is meant to bond people who share the same delight. It brings people together. Laughter is supposed to **unite** people. We laugh **with** our friends when we share a joyful moment.

If a person laughs **at** another person, though, his body twists the God-given meaning of laughter. This laughter **divides** people. Bullies often laugh at others, not as an expression of joy, but of contempt, and when they do this, their bodies tell lies.

Which picture shows the truth of the meaning of laughter? Which shows a lie?

Truth Twisters

We can think of many examples from books and films of how the body does not always speak the truth. In the fairy tale of *Snow White*, the wicked queen disguises herself as an old woman and gives Snow White a beautiful apple. The queen's body says, *I am trustworthy.* However, the apple is poisoned, so it is not a gift at all, but a means to hurt Snow White.

Each time Lucy holds the football for Charlie Brown in the famous *Peanuts* comics, her body speaks a language. It says, *You can trust me. I am helping you.* But each time he tries to kick it, she pulls the football away at the last minute, and Charlie Brown flies up in the air and falls. Lucy's body tells a lie. It speaks falsely to Charlie Brown and betrays his trust and friendship.

Aesop shows how the body can tell a lie in the fable, *The Boy Who Cried Wolf*. To amuse himself, a shepherd boy ran to his village and frantically cried, "Help! A wolf is attacking the sheep!"

His spoken lie was believable because his body showed fear. So the villagers came to help. When they saw it was a trick, they were angry. The boy did this again later, and again the villagers were angered. When a real wolf attacked the sheep, the boy ran and again cried, "Wolf! Wolf!" But this time the villagers did not believe him and did not help.

Like the boy in the fable, we lose people's trust when we lie through our words or with the language of the body. We earn the trust of our parents, teachers, and friends when we speak truth with our bodies as well as with our words.

Examples from the Bible

Scripture, too, shows examples of telling lies with the body. In the Old Testament (before the time of Christ), Jacob pretended to be his older brother, Esau, in order to get his father's blessing. His father's eyesight was poor, so smooth-skinned Jacob put goatskins on his arms to be more like his hairier brother. When his father felt Jacob's arms, his father believed that he was giving his blessing to Esau. Jacob's body spoke a lie.

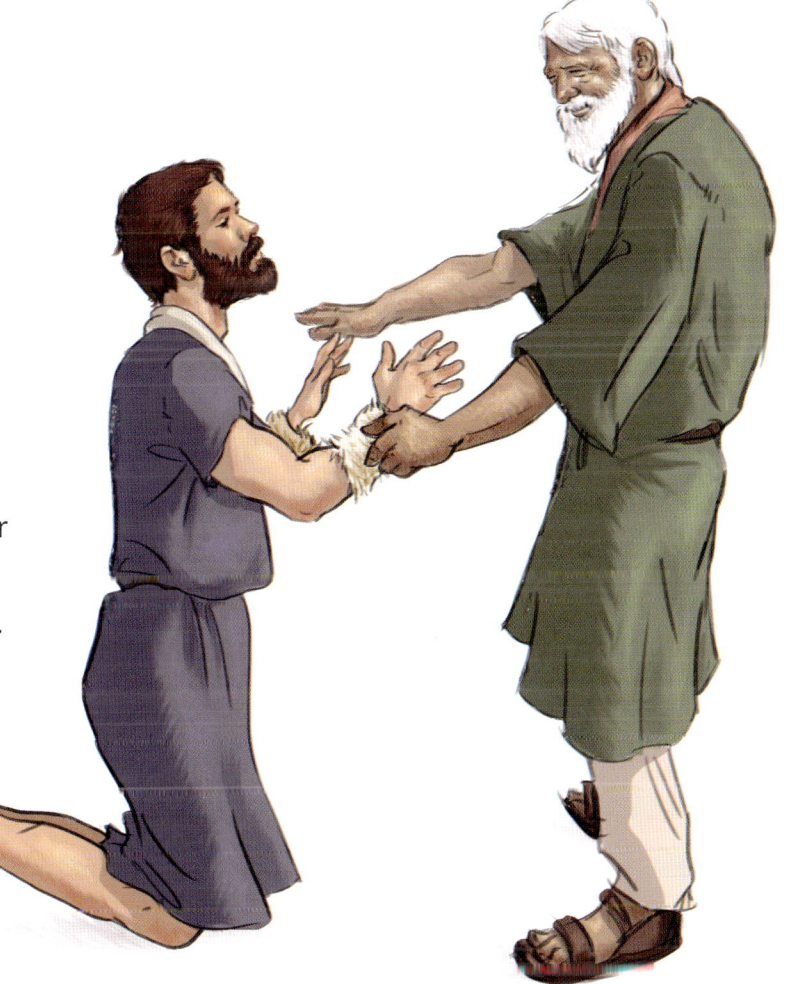

Judas' body spoke the worst lie in all of history. To identify Our Lord to the soldiers, Judas betrayed Jesus with a kiss. A kiss is a sign of love and faithfulness. With a kiss, the body says, *We are close, like family.* But Judas' kiss was a lie. It meant, *I am pretending to be your friend.* But the truth was that Judas saw Jesus as his enemy.

"Jesus said to him, 'Judas, are you betraying the Son of Man with a kiss?'" (Luke 22:48)

"...[T]he body tells the truth through faithfulness... and when... it tells a lie, it commits falsehood."

Theology of the Body 104:8

Know the Truth, Show the Truth

Because there is a deep, God-given meaning behind bodily actions, we should be careful that our bodies always speak the truth.

Tears, for example, call forth compassion from others. If you are hurt or sad and show it with tears, your body is speaking the truth. Have you heard of crocodile tears? That's when people cry to get sympathy or attention, not because they are truly sorrowful. Their bodies say, *I am sad—comfort me!* Yet they are not truly sad. Their bodies are not speaking the truth.

When a child is sick and shows it by staying in bed, her body speaks the truth. But if that child stays in bed only pretending to be sick so that she doesn't have to go to school, her body is not speaking the truth.

When a student turns in his own work, his body speaks the truth. If he turns in work with answers copied from someone else, his body speaks a lie. By putting his name on it and turning in the assignment to the teacher, his body says, *This is my work,* which he knows to be false.

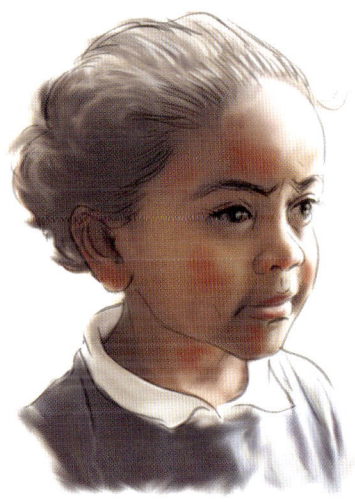

Let us honor God's gift of the body and the way He designed us to communicate truth. When our bodily actions match what we know to reflect a God-given meaning, we give and receive trust. A smile, a frown, a grimace, and a glance all send truthful messages when they are sincere. Speaking truthfully with our bodies creates strong friendships, loving families, and happy people.

"...Since God is 'true,' the members of his people are called to live in the truth...."   *CCC 2465*

Mission: When you are tempted to tell a lie with words or the body, make the Sign of the Cross with your thumb over your lips, to remind yourself to act in truth.

3 Manners and the Truth

Gold Rush to Truth

Sometimes in order to be lovingly polite, we need to be careful when we speak the truth. It is best not to act on our first thoughts or feelings. This does not mean we should be untruthful.

Like a miner digging for gold, we need to search for the greatest truth and not fall victim to the "false-gold" or incomplete truths.

"...The inner man is *called by Christ to... distinguish and judge the various movements of his own heart.... This task can* be carried out and... it is truly worthy of man." *Theology of the Body 48:4*

Manners Around the World

Our bodies speak the language of politeness in order to reveal truth with charity.

Good manners are important and valued in cultures around the world. They are a sign of respect among human beings. When we use good manners, our bodies speak this language of respect.

People show politeness with their bodies in different ways around the world.

In Japan, it is polite to bow, rather than shake hands, when you meet someone. In Ethiopia, it is polite to eat rice with your fingers. In China, it is impolite to receive a gift with just one hand. In Pakistan, it would be bad manners to eat with your left hand. In Nepal, it is polite to take your shoes off when you enter someone's home; if you leave them on, it is impolite.

Your Manners

Our bodies can speak the language of politeness. Perhaps you have been taught the following ways to show good manners.

We knock before entering a room to protect the privacy of others.

We say "excuse me" to the people around us when trying to squeeze by in a crowd. With these words, we are asking them to forgive the discomfort or inconvenience we may cause.

We make eye contact with others when listening to them. This lets them know that we see them, that they are important, and that we think their words are important.

We sit quietly and patiently among adults, even if we are bored. This shows respect for the event, for the adults, and for ourselves.

When it comes to good manners, there is so much to remember...

Make eye contact!

Cover my mouth when I sneeze!

Don't snoop in other people's things!

Never interrupt a speaker!

Share my toys!

Say please and thank you!

Don't talk with a full mouth!

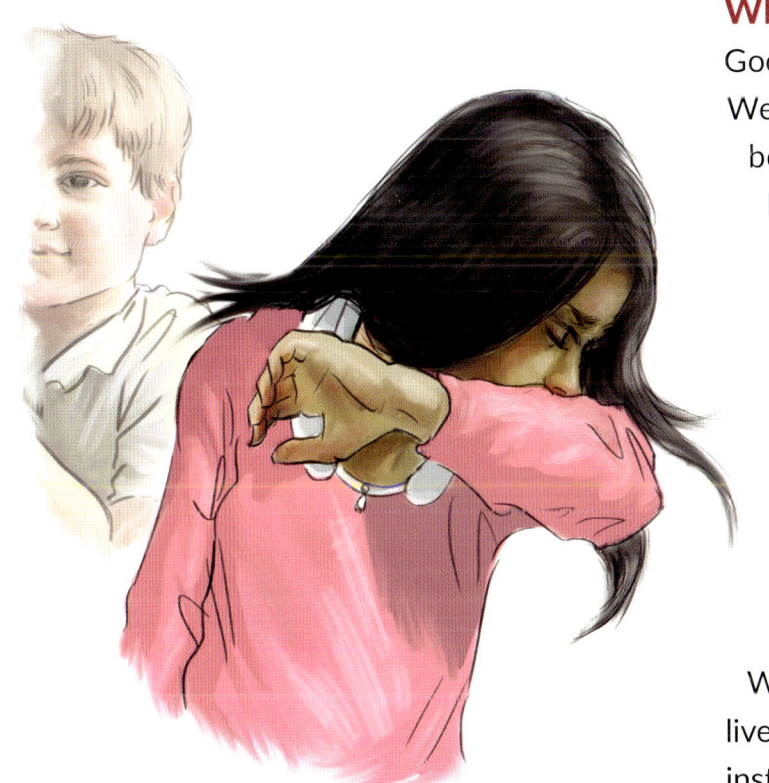

Why Do We Need Good Manners?

Good manners show love for our neighbors. We practice good manners with our bodies as a way of showing respect. People live in greater peace with each other when they use polite manners.

A girl can protect her friend from germs when she turns her head to cough.

A boy can help a young mother pushing a heavy stroller by running to open a door for her.

We can give our family a nice, tidy place to live when we put our muddy shoes outside instead of leaving them on the kitchen floor.

31

Good manners can mean doing certain things, like using polite words or offering your seat to someone. But they also mean not doing certain things.

We know that a young child should **not** shout, "That guy is so fat!" or "That lady is so old!" Why not? The child may be speaking truth, after all. Yet, politeness reminds us that being kind is more important than announcing every truth that comes into our heads.

Controlling our impulses is an important part of politeness. We need to restrain our bodies from speaking when it's inappropriate. There are times when our bodies should be silent.

The Golden Rule

Sometimes the plain truth can be hurtful. Hurting others unnecessarily is contrary to good manners and contrary to our Christian Faith. Remember the Golden Rule:

Do unto others as you would have them do unto you.

We can learn to be both truthful **and** kind. Goodness and truth belong together.

When my friend brings candy in her lunch, I might immediately beg her to share it with me. Why would that impulse be impolite?

When I feel tired at school in the afternoon, I want to put my head down on the desk to rest. Why would that impulse be impolite?

What Would You Do?

Aunt Gertrude hands you a Christmas gift, and it's... a pair of socks! You are not excited about this gift, yet instead of frowning and tossing the socks aside, you allow your body to speak the language of politeness by thanking Aunt Gertrude for her gift.

Your body did not express the smaller truth of your disappointment. Instead, you told the greater truth of your respect for your aunt. You protected her feelings and your family bond. You chose to speak the language of good manners.

You are at your friend Anna's house, having dinner with her family. There is one brownie left on the plate for dessert, and you want it. You know that some people haven't had a brownie yet, and you have already had one. They offer it to you, but you politely shake your head and say, "Oh, no, thank you. The brownie I already had was delicious."

Why did you respond this way? You did not choose to speak the smaller truth, which was your appetite or desire for the last brownie.

Instead, you chose to speak the greater truth of your generosity. You left the brownie in a spirit of sharing; you put the needs of others before yourself. Your body spoke the language of politeness.

I would love to eat that brownie, but Noah hasn't had one yet…

No, thank you.

The Body Shows Respect

When I write a thank-you note for a birthday gift, I show good manners. My body speaks a language of gratitude.

When I see my father enter the room, I acknowledge his presence. My father is more important than the video game I'm playing. I show good manners by turning toward him and turning away from the video game.

Good manners are rooted in gratitude and appreciation of others. We are thankful to God for creating the people we meet in the world. Our bodies show this thankfulness and respect when they speak the language of good manners.

When we find the greatest truth in each situation and express it in a loving way, our bodies speak the language of politeness.

"...[C]harity always proceeds by way of respect for one's neighbor and his conscience...."
CCC 1789

Mission: See if your body can speak the language of politeness at least three times today. Hold the door open for someone, let another person go ahead of you, or say "please" and "thank you."

4 The Body Speaks in Scripture

The Language of the Body in Scripture

Thank God for language! We need words! In fact, words are so important that Scripture says in John 1:1, "In the beginning was the Word, and the Word was with God, and the Word was God." St. John uses the expression "The Word" to refer to God the Son, the Second Person of the Blessed Trinity.

Spoken and written language is made up of words. Words have power and meaning. God gave us another language too. The body's language also has power and meaning.

Have you heard the well-known saying that we should preach the Gospel at all times and only use words if necessary? How can we preach the Gospel without using words?

With our bodies!

We can look at salvation history to see examples of how the human body has spoken through time.

Joyful Language

When King David brought the Ark of the Covenant into the holy city of Jerusalem, he danced for joy before it! His body said, *I am glad You are here, my God, and I rejoice in You.*

When Mary visited her cousin Elizabeth, both were pregnant. Even in his mother's womb, John the Baptist sensed Jesus' nearness and he leapt for joy. John's tiny body spoke a language, echoing the words of King David, *I am glad You are here, my God, and I rejoice in You.*

Reverent Language

Scripture shows ways that the body speaks the God-given truth in the heart. One way we show honor to a king is by bowing. We bow before God because He is our King.

The Magi bowed down to the Child Jesus, and they laid costly gifts before Him. Without words, their bodies prayed, *You are our King. We give You homage.*

After the miraculous catch of fish, Peter recognized Christ as his Savior. He said to Jesus, "Depart from me, Lord, for I am a sinful man." His body echoed this as he knelt. His body said truthfully, *I am small; You are great. I am not worthy.*

Trusting Language

A woman suffering from an incurable ailment approached Jesus in a crowd. She knew that even His slightest touch could heal. She stretched out her hand in faith to touch the tassel of His robe. Her body said, *I believe, Lord*, and she was cured.

Another Gospel story tells of the sisters Martha and Mary whom Jesus and His disciples were visiting. Martha was busy cleaning, cooking, and serving. Her body spoke the truth of her heart which was, *I love the Lord by working for Him*. Her sister Mary sat at Jesus' feet and listened to Him. Her body spoke the truth too, saying, *I love the Lord in quiet adoration.*

Lying Language

The Bible also shows that it is possible to tell a lie with the body by twisting the God-given meanings of certain bodily actions.

During Jesus' Passion, a group of Roman guards performed actions that were normally meant to honor a king: they dressed Him in purple robes, put a scepter in His hand, and placed a crown on His head. But the robes were meant to mock Him, the scepter was a reed, and the crown was made of painful thorns.

They then knelt in front of Him and called out, "Hail, King of the Jews!" Their kneeling, however, did not show reverence. The guards were taunting and bullying Jesus by twisting the truth of the body.

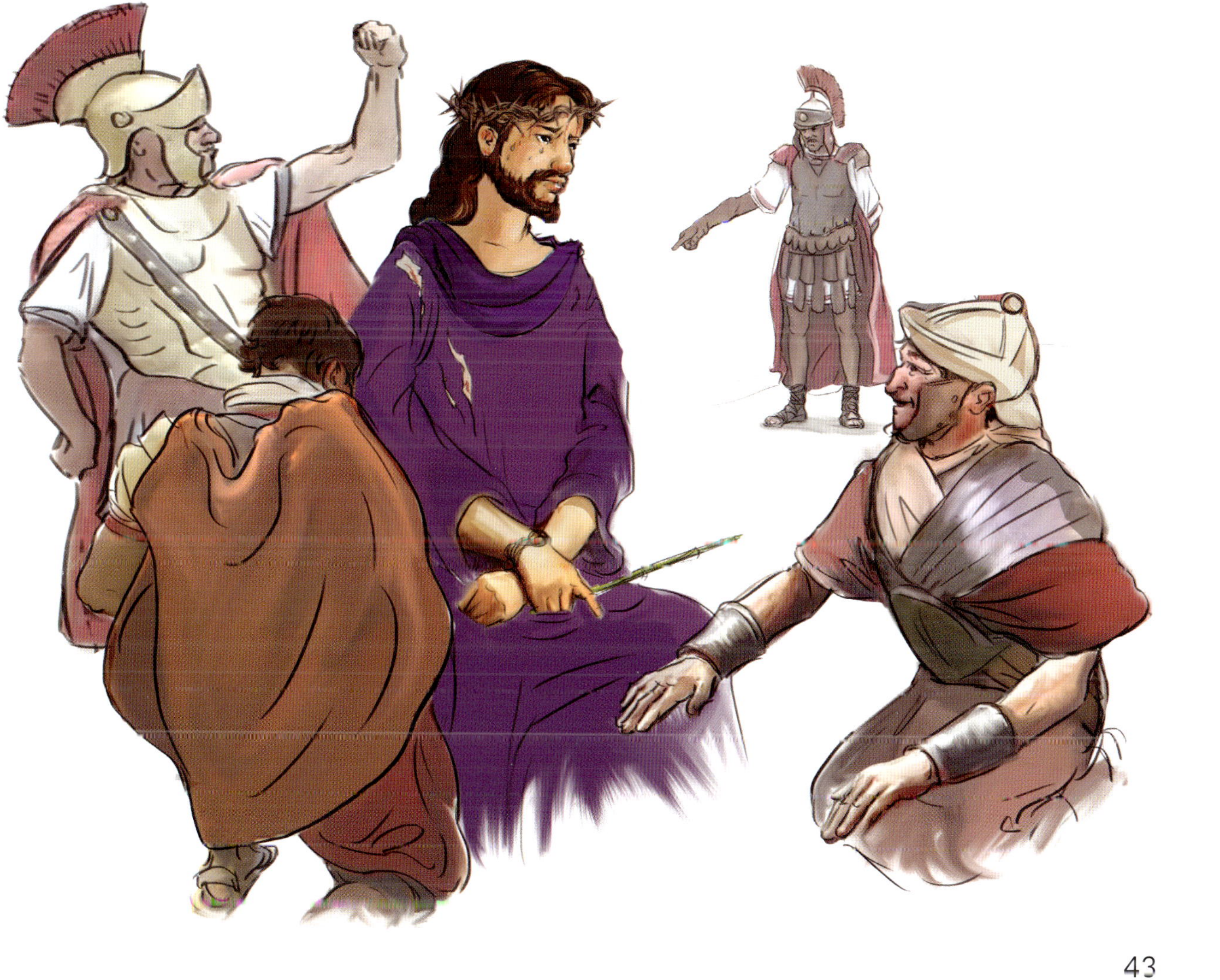

Love Language

Good manners were as important in Biblical times as they are today. It was the custom for a host to offer his guests water to wash their dusty feet. This custom was neglected when Jesus went to a Pharisee's home for dinner. However, a repentant woman found Jesus there. She washed His feet with tears of gratitude for His mercy. She dried His feet with her hair and anointed them with costly oil. The language of her body went beyond the simple courtesy of the foot-washing. She expressed a gift of love to her Lord. Her body said to Him, *I am sorry for doing wrong. I offer You my whole self.*

The Language of Jesus' Body

The Gospels show that the goodness of Jesus is rooted in truth. Our Lord always knew the greatest truth and spoke it with His body.

He did not avoid those with the terrible disease of leprosy; He touched them and healed them out of love.

Even when Our Lord was hungry and weary, instead of resting, He stood and preached tirelessly of the Father's love, because the people needed this Good News so badly.

He held the hand of a little girl who had died and raised her back to life to show that He has power over death.

After His Resurrection, Jesus cooked breakfast on the shore for His beloved disciples to show them that He is fully alive and still caring for them.

At the Last Supper, Jesus broke bread and offered it, saying, "This is My Body, which will be given for you." The very next day, His Body was again broken and offered for us when He suffered on the cross.

The Language of Mary's Body

Likewise, Mary's body spoke volumes as she stood at the foot of the cross. Even when her heart felt pierced with pain, she did not run away. She stayed and suffered through every moment of Jesus' Passion with Him. The language of Mary's body said, *I am with You no matter what. I share Your love and pain, which saves the world. I love You.*

Jesus' Body Speaks to You

If we consider Jesus on the cross, what does His Body say to us?

His arms are outstretched, saying, *I offer all that I have. I want to embrace you all!*

His Body hangs vertically on the cross, saying, *I am the link between Heaven and Earth. I bring God's forgiveness to you.*

His gaze is directed toward the Earth, saying, *I look upon you with love and mercy.*

He is the Word.

His Body speaks eternally.

47

> "God could not show his love more forcefully than by allowing himself in the person of the Son to be nailed to the Cross for us."   *see YOUCAT 101*

CATHOLIC TREASURE BOX

The Body Speaks Liturgical Language

Our bodies speak a language always—even at Mass!

We **stand** to show respect, attention, and honor. We **sit** to show that we are listening and meditating. We **kneel and are quiet** to show reverence and humility before God. We **make the Sign of the Cross** to remind ourselves of both the Blessed Trinity and the Crucifixion of Our Lord. It is also a way to remember our Baptism. Through our **bodily actions**, we show peace and goodwill to our fellow brothers and sisters in Christ at Mass.